100 facts
Bugs

100 facts
Bugs

Steve Parker
Consultants: Dr. Jim Flegg

Miles
Kelly

First published in 2001 by Miles Kelly Publishing Ltd
Harding's Barn, Bardfield End Green, Thaxted, Essex, CM6 3PX, UK

This updated edition printed in 2015

2 4 6 8 10 9 7 5 3 1

Publishing Director Belinda Gallagher
Creative Director Jo Cowan
Editor Fran Bromage
Designers Rob Hale, D&A Design
Image Manager Liberty Newton
Indexer Jane Parker
Production Elizabeth Collins, Caroline Kelly
Reprographics Stephan Davis, Jennifer Cozens, Thom Allaway

ISBN 978-1-78209-935-2

Printed in China

British Library Cataloging-in-Publication Data
A catalog record for this book is available from the British Library

ACKNOWLEDGMENTS
The publishers would like to thank the following sources for the use of their photographs:
Key: t = top, b = bottom, l = left, r = right, c = center, bg = background

Cover: (front) Rob Hainer/Shutterstock.com; (back) Daniel Prudek/Shutterstock.com,
(cl) CathyKeifer/iStockphoto.com **Dreamstime** 35(bc) Paop; 40(c) Cathy Keifer **FLPA** 24(t) Bob Gibbons;
27(bc) Christian Ziegler/Minden Pictures; 32(bc) Alfred Schauhuber/Imagebroker; 37(b) Albert Visage
Glow Images 6(c) F. Rauschenbach/F1online; 23(c) Rolf Nussbaumer; 25(cl) Meul, J./Arco Images GmbH;
39(tc) Meul, J./Arco Images GmbH **iStock** 11(tr) Cathy Keifer; 34(c) Paija **Nature Picture Library** 10(tr) Meul/
ARCO; 13(bl) Nature Production; 14(c) Stephen Dalton; 15(tl) Stephen Dalton; 17(c) Visuals Unlimited;
30(r) John Cancalosi; 43(b) Kim Taylor **Shutterstock.com** 1(c) Marco Uliana; 2(bg) Sean van Tonder; 5(tl) Mirek
Kijewski, (tr) Andrey Burmakin, (b) Kletr; 9(r) Tan Hung Meng; 11(bc) Geanina Bechea; 12(bg) Aleksandr Kurganov,
(bl) jps, (c) Marco Uliana; 14(bg) Triff; 15(br) Mark Carrel; 16(c) Smit; 18(tr) Sue Robinson; 19(tr) Dirk Ercken;
20(bg) fotoslaz; 21(br) Steve Byland; 22(tr) jcwait; 24(bg) Jorge Moro, (bl) dabjola, (cl) Rasmus Holmboe Dahl;
25(tr) Nick Stubbs, (bc) Henrik Larsson; 29(tl) Csati; 31(cl) Matt Jeppson, (t) IrinaK, (bl) Narisa Koryanyong;
32(bg) Triff; 33(cr) xpixel, (cl) Glenn Jenkinson; 36(bg) Dr. Morley Read, (c) Eric Isselee; 38(cl) r. classen;
42(bl) Lidara; 44(bl) Cosmin Manci; 45(tc) blewisphotography; 46(c) LilKar; 47(bl) npouard Rozey
Science Photo Library 37(b) Thomas & Pat Leeson

All other photographs are from: digitalSTOCK, Fotolia, PhotoDisc, Stockbyte

The publishers would like to thank Stuart Jackson-Carter for the artwork he contributed to this book.

All other artwork from the Miles Kelly Artwork Bank

Every effort has been made to acknowledge the source and copyright holder of each picture
Miles Kelly Publishing apologizes for any unintentional errors or omissions

Made with paper from a sustainable forest

www.mileskelly.net
info@mileskelly.net

The publishers would like to thank the Royal Entomological Society
for their help in compiling this book.

Contents

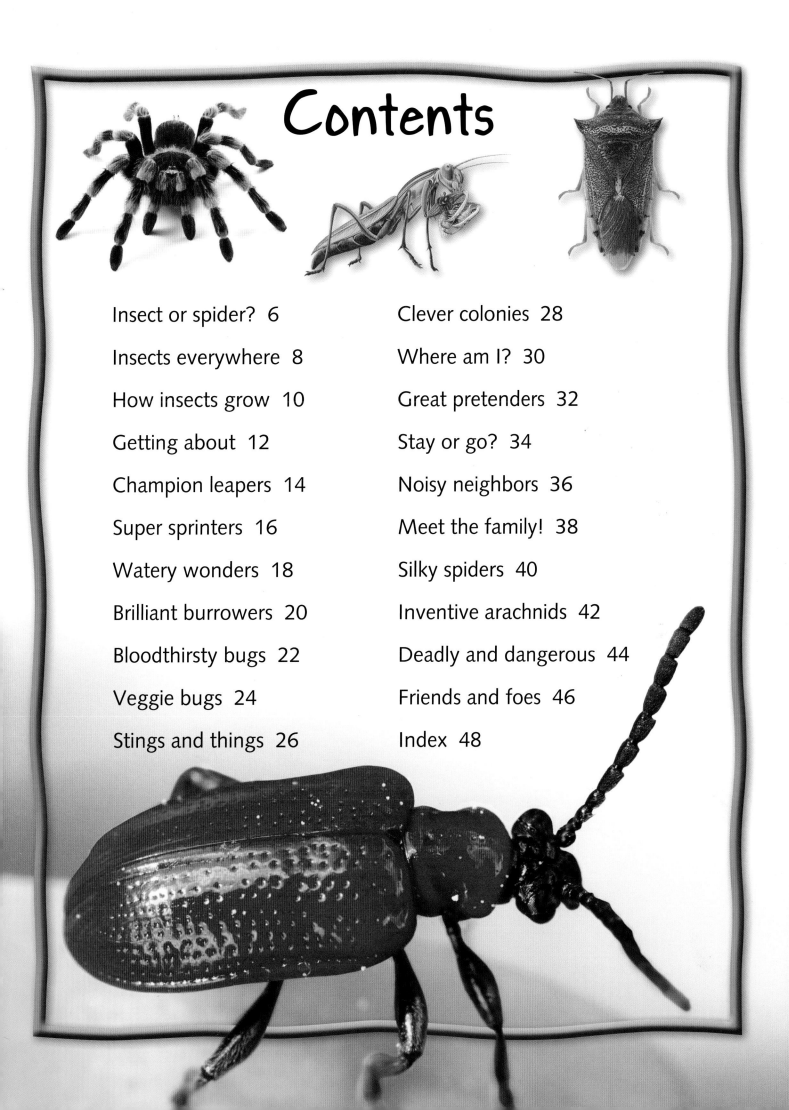

Insect or spider?

1 Insects are among the most numerous and widespread animals on Earth. They form the largest of all animal groups, with millions of different kinds, or species, which live almost everywhere in the world. But not all creepy-crawlies are insects. Spiders belong to a different group called arachnids, and millipedes are in yet another group.

▶ Cockchafers are insects, as shown by their wings and six legs. Also called chafers, cockchafers belong to the largest subgroup of insects, the beetles.

Insects everywhere

2 **The housefly is one of the most common, widespread, and annoying insects.** There are many other members of the fly group, such as bluebottles, horseflies, craneflies, and fruitflies. They all have two wings. Most other kinds of insects have four wings.

3 **The ladybug is a noticeable insect with its bright red or yellow body, and black spots.** It is a member of the beetle group—the biggest insect group of all. There are more than half a million kinds, from massive Goliath beetles to tiny flea beetles.

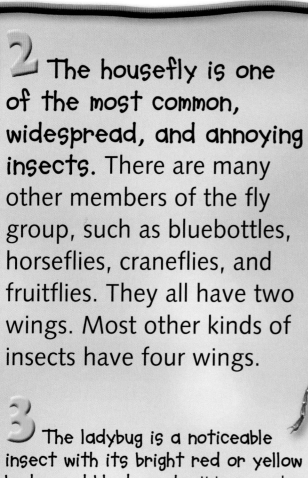

▶ Bright colors warn other animals that ladybugs taste horrible.

4 **The earwig is a familiar insect outside —and sometimes inside.** Despite their name, earwigs do not crawl into ears or hide in wigs, but they do like dark, damp corners. Earwigs form one of the smaller insect groups, with fewer than 2,000 different kinds.

▼ Insects, such as this horsefly, do not have a bony skeleton like we do. Their bodies are covered by horny plates, called an exoskeleton.

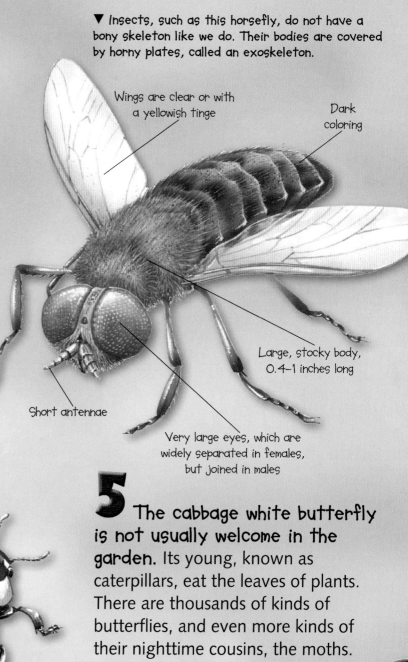

Wings are clear or with a yellowish tinge

Dark coloring

Large, stocky body, 0.4–1 inches long

Short antennae

Very large eyes, which are widely separated in females, but joined in males

5 **The cabbage white butterfly is not usually welcome in the garden.** Its young, known as caterpillars, eat the leaves of plants. There are thousands of kinds of butterflies, and even more kinds of their nighttime cousins, the moths.

▼ When the earwig is threatened, it raises its tail to try to make itself look bigger.

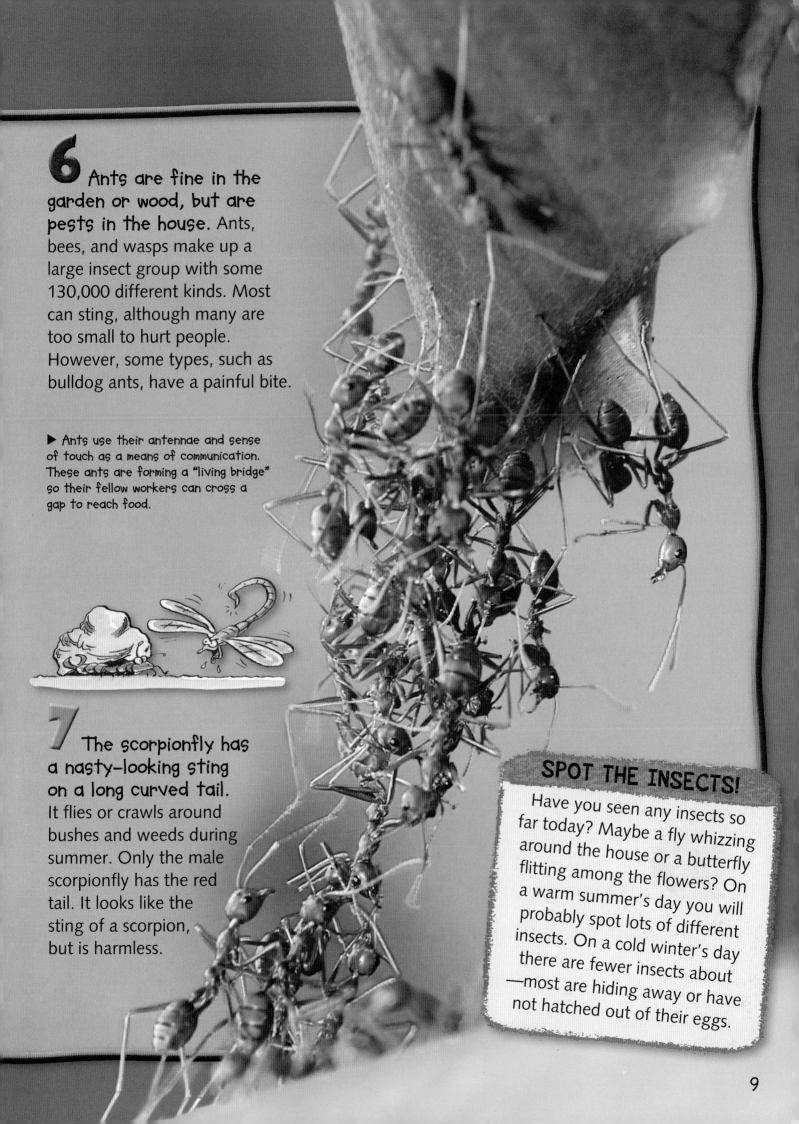

6 Ants are fine in the garden or wood, but are pests in the house. Ants, bees, and wasps make up a large insect group with some 130,000 different kinds. Most can sting, although many are too small to hurt people. However, some types, such as bulldog ants, have a painful bite.

▶ Ants use their antennae and sense of touch as a means of communication. These ants are forming a "living bridge" so their fellow workers can cross a gap to reach food.

7 The scorpionfly has a nasty-looking sting on a long curved tail. It flies or crawls around bushes and weeds during summer. Only the male scorpionfly has the red tail. It looks like the sting of a scorpion, but is harmless.

SPOT THE INSECTS!

Have you seen any insects so far today? Maybe a fly whizzing around the house or a butterfly flitting among the flowers? On a warm summer's day you will probably spot lots of different insects. On a cold winter's day there are fewer insects about —most are hiding away or have not hatched out of their eggs.

How insects grow

8 Nearly all insects begin life inside an egg. The female insect usually lays her eggs in an out-of-the-way place, such as under a stone, leaf, or bark, or in the soil.

▼ The scarlet lily beetle lays her eggs directly onto the lily leaves, which the grubs will eat when they hatch.

9 Usually a female insect mates with a male insect before she can lay her eggs. The female and male come together to check they are both the same kind of insect and are healthy. This is known as courtship. Butterflies often flit through the air together in a "courtship dance."

10 When some types of insects hatch, they do not look like their parents. A young beetle, butterfly, or fly is soft-bodied, wriggly, and wormlike. This young stage is called a larva. A beetle larva is called a grub, a butterfly larva is a caterpillar, and a fly larva is a maggot.

◀ Large caterpillars always eat into the center of the leaf from the edge. Caterpillars grasp the leaf with their legs, while their specially developed front jaws chew their food.

1. The butterfly swallows air, expands its body, and splits its chrysalis open

2. It struggles free of the casing

3. The butterfly clings to the chrysalis

4. Blood is pumped into the wings, which stretch and stiffen

5. In half an hour, the wings are full size. Once dry, the butterfly is able to fly

▲ This viceroy butterfly is emerging from its chrysalis.

11 **The larva eats and eats.** It sheds its skin several times so it can grow. Then it changes into the next stage of its life, called a pupa. The pupa has a hard outer case that stays still and inactive. Inside, the larva is changing shape again—this is known as metamorphosis.

12 **At last the pupa's case splits open and the adult insect crawls out.** Its body, legs, and wings spread out and harden. Now the insect is ready to find food and a mate.

13 **Some kinds of insects change shape less as they grow.** When a cricket or grasshopper hatches, it looks similar to its parents, but it may not have wings.

14 **The young cricket eats and eats, and sheds (or molts) its skin several times as it grows.** Each time it looks more like its parent. A young insect that resembles an adult is called a nymph. At the last molt it becomes a fully formed adult, ready to feed and breed.

◄ Most crickets, as well as grasshoppers and locusts, molt between five and eight times before adulthood.

Getting about

15 An insect's wings are attached to the middle part of its body, the thorax. This is like a box with strong walls, called a clickbox. Muscles pull to make the walls click in and out, which in turn makes the wings flick up and down. A large butterfly flaps its wings once or twice each second. Some tiny flies flap almost 1,000 times each second.

16 Most kinds of insects have two pairs of wings and use them to fly from place to place. One of the strongest fliers is the Apollo butterfly of Europe and Asia. It flies high over hills and mountains, then rests on a rock or flower in the sunshine.

17 The smallest fliers include gnats, midges, and mosquitoes. These are true flies, with one pair of wings. Some are almost too tiny for us to see. Certain types bite animals and people, sucking their blood as food.

◄ Apollo butterflies flit between plants, searching for sweet nectar to drink.

18 A few insects lack wings. They are mostly very small and live in the soil, such as bristletails and certain aphids. One kind of bristletail is the silverfish—a small, shiny, fast-running insect.

▲ Dragonflies catch prey in a "basket" formed by their legs.

► Silverfish are nocturnal, which means they are mainly active at night.

19 A fast and fierce flying hunter is the dragonfly. Its huge eyes spot tiny prey such as midges and mayflies. The dragonfly dashes through the air, turns at speed, grabs the victim, and flies back to a perch to eat its meal.

20 Some insects flash bright lights as they fly. The firefly is not a fly, but a type of beetle. Male fireflies "dance" in the air at dusk, the rear parts of their bodies glowing on and off about once each second. Female fireflies stay on twigs and leaves, and glow in reply as part of their courtship.

▼ Each kind of firefly has its own pattern of flashes.

QUIZ

1. How many wings do most insects have?
2. Where on its body are an insect's wings attached?
3. Which part of the firefly glows in the dark?

Answers:
1. Two pairs
2. Its middle, called the thorax
3. Rear parts

Champion leapers

21 Many insects move around mainly by hopping and jumping, rather than flying. They have long, strong legs and can leap great distances, especially to avoid enemies and escape from danger. Grasshoppers are up to 6 inches long and some types can jump more than 10 foot. The grasshopper often opens its brightly patterned wings briefly as it leaps, giving a flash of color.

22 The springtail jumps with its tail, rather than its legs. The rear part of its body is shaped like a V or Y. It is folded under the body until it flicks down and flips the insect through the air. Springtails are as long as this letter "I" but some can leap more than 2 inches!

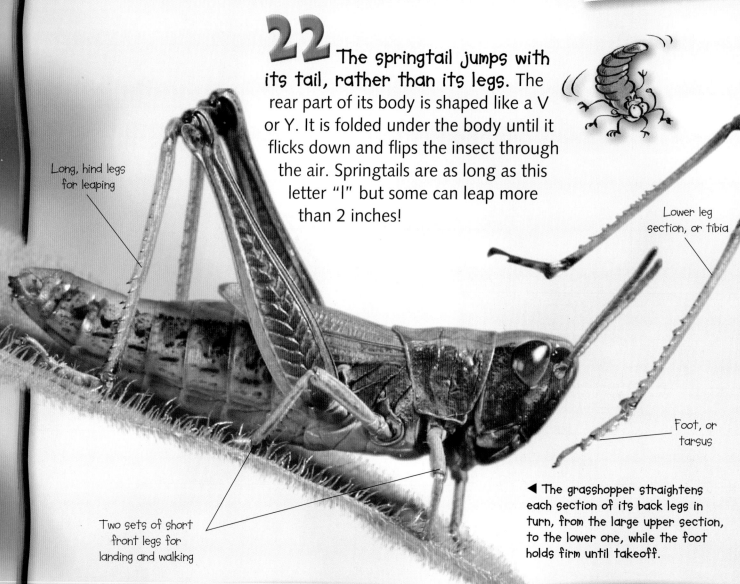

Long, hind legs for leaping

Lower leg section, or tibia

Foot, or tarsus

Two sets of short front legs for landing and walking

◄ The grasshopper straightens each section of its back legs in turn, from the large upper section, to the lower one, while the foot holds firm until takeoff.

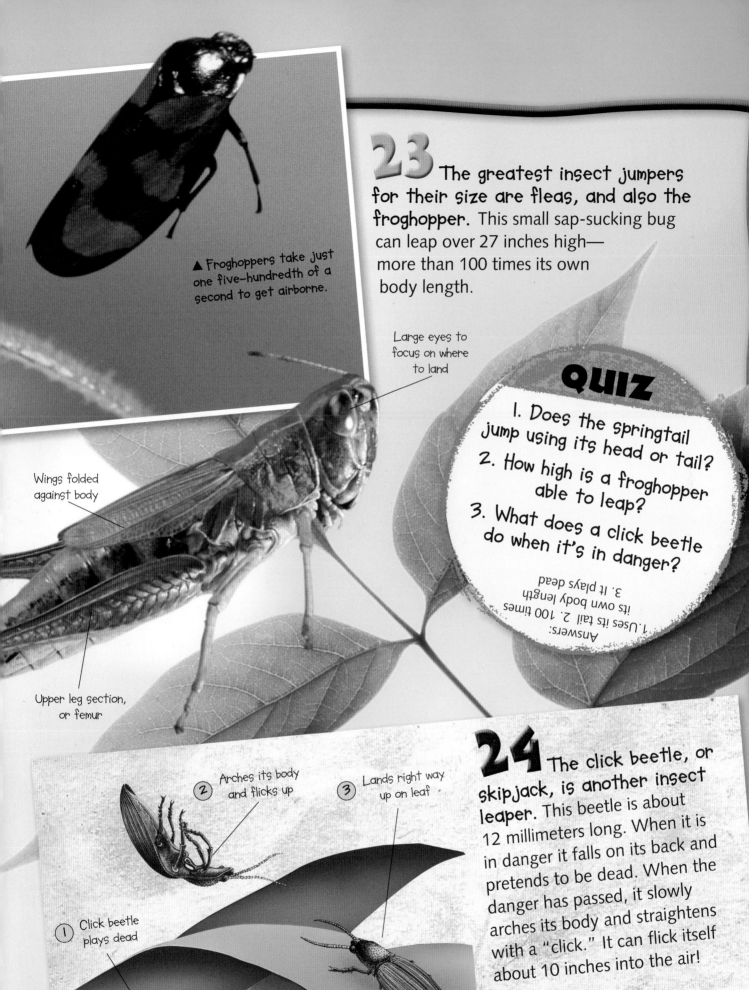

▲ Froghoppers take just one five-hundredth of a second to get airborne.

23 The greatest insect jumpers for their size are fleas, and also the froghopper. This small sap-sucking bug can leap over 27 inches high—more than 100 times its own body length.

Large eyes to focus on where to land

Wings folded against body

Upper leg section, or femur

QUIZ

1. Does the springtail jump using its head or tail?
2. How high is a froghopper able to leap?
3. What does a click beetle do when it's in danger?

Answers:
1. Uses its tail 2. 100 times its own body length 3. It plays dead

② Arches its body and flicks up

③ Lands right way up on leaf

① Click beetle plays dead

24 The click beetle, or skipjack, is another insect leaper. This beetle is about 12 millimeters long. When it is in danger it falls on its back and pretends to be dead. When the danger has passed, it slowly arches its body and straightens with a "click." It can flick itself about 10 inches into the air!

◀ The "click" is from a joint between the first and second thorax parts.

15

Super sprinters

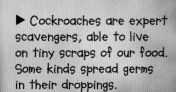

▶ Cockroaches are expert
scavengers, able to live
on tiny scraps of our food.
Some kinds spread germs
in their droppings.

25 Some insects rarely fly or
leap. They prefer to run and run...
all day, and sometimes all night too.
Among the champion insect runners
are cockroaches. There are about
4,500 different kinds and they are
tough and adaptable. Some live
in soil or caves, but most scurry
speedily across the ground and dart
into narrow crevices, under logs,
stones, cupboards—even beds!

26 One of the busiest insect walkers is the devil's coach-horse, which resembles an earwig. It belongs to the group known as rove beetles, which walk huge distances to find food.

▼ The devil's coach-horse has powerful mouthparts to tear apart small caterpillars, grubs, and worms.

27 Some insects can run along smooth slippery surfaces, such as walls, windows, or wet rocks. Others can run along the beds of ponds and rivers. The stonefly nymph has big, strong, wide-splayed legs that grip even smooth stones in rushing streams.

◄ The stonefly nymph, the larva of the stonefly, scuttles over wet rocks and riverbeds searching for food.

28 The green tiger beetle is an active hunter. It races over open ground, chasing smaller creatures such as ants, woodlice, worms, and little spiders. It has huge jaws for its size and rips apart any victim.

I DON'T BELIEVE IT!

Green tiger beetles are about 12–15 millimeters long but can run at about 24–28 inches per second. That is like a human sprinter running 100 meters in one second!

Watery wonders

▶ Pondskaters row on water with their rear four legs.

29 Many kinds of insects live underwater in ponds, streams, rivers, and lakes. Some walk along the bottom, others swim strongly using their legs as oars to row through the water. The great diving beetle hunts small water creatures, such as tadpoles and baby fish. It can give a person a painful bite in self-defense.

30 Some insects even walk on water. The pondskater has a slim, light body with long, wide-splayed legs. It glides across the water surface "skin" or film, known as surface tension. The pondskater is a member of the bug group of insects and eats tiny animals that fall into the pond.

▶ The great diving beetle breathes air, which it collects and stores under the hard wing-cases on its back.

Large pincerlike mouthparts

INVESTIGATE

With help from a grown-up, fill a bowl of water and let the water settle. Investigate what you can place on top of the water that doesn't break the water tension. Try laying paper, plastic, or grass on the water. What happens?

Partly formed wings

◄ A damselfly nymph hunts tiny water creatures, including other insect nymphs.

Smooth, hard wing-cases keeps the beetle streamlined

Feathery gills

Hairs on legs help the diving beetle to swim

31 The nymphs of dragonflies, damselflies, stoneflies, and mayflies have tails with feathery gills. These work like the gills of a fish, and help the nymph breath underwater. These young insects do not need to go to the surface until they change into adults.

32 Some water insects, such as the great silver water beetle, breathe air. They must come to the surface for fresh air supplies. The hairs on the beetle's body then trap tiny bubbles of air for breathing below.

Brilliant burrowers

33 Soil teems with millions of creatures—and many are insects. Some are larvae or grubs, others are full-grown insects, such as burrowing beetles, ants, termites, and earwigs. These soil insects are a vital source of food for all kinds of larger animals, from spiders and shrews to moles and birds.

34 The larva of the click beetle is shiny orange, up to 25 millimeters long and called a **wireworm**. It stays undergound, feeding on plant parts, for up to five years. Then it changes into an adult and leaves the soil. Wireworms can be serious pests of crops such as barley, oats, wheat, potatoes, and beet.

▶ Many insects pose a threat to farmers' crops. Farmers can use pesticides—chemicals to kill the insects—but many people think that this harms other plants and animals.

35

The larva of the cranefly ("daddy longlegs") is called a leatherjacket because of its tough, leathery skin. Leatherjackets eat the roots of grasses, including cereal crops, such as wheat. They hatch from their eggs in late summer and feed in the soil. They change into pupae and then adults the following summer.

INSECT LARVAE

1. African fruit beetle larva
2. Black cutworm caterpillar
3. Cicada grub
4. Click beetle larva
5. Cockchafer grub
6. Leatherjacket
7. Japanese beetle larva

ADULT INSECTS

1. African fruit beetle
2. Black cutworm moth
3. Cicada
4. Click beetle
5. Cockchafer
6. Cranefly
7. Japanese beetle

36

The larva of the cicada may live underground for more than ten years. Different types of cicadas stay in the soil for different periods of time. The American periodic cicada is probably the record holder, taking 17 years to change into a pupa and then an adult. Adults make loud chirping or buzzing sounds.

▶ Adult cicadas suck the sap of bushes and trees.

Bloodthirsty bugs

37 Although most insects are small, they are among the fiercest hunters in the animal world. Many have huge mouthparts shaped like spears or saws, for grabbing and tearing up victims. Some actively chase after prey, while others lie in wait and surprise it.

Powerful jaws for digging and cutting up food

▲ Insect jaws, or mandibles, like this wasp's, move from side-to-side.

38 The antlion larva digs small pits in sand or loose soil. It hides below the surface at the bottom of the pit and waits for small creatures to wander past and slip in. The larva then grasps them with its fanglike mouthparts.

39 The lacewing looks delicate and dainty, but it is a fearsome hunter. It hunts aphids such as greenfly and blackfly, and drinks their body fluids. It may also have a sip of sweet, sugary nectar from a flower.

▼ The lacewing is green to blend in with the leaves where it hunts.

40 One of the most powerful insect predators is the praying mantis. It gets its name from the way it holds its front legs folded, like a person with hands together in prayer. The front legs have sharp spines, and snap together like spiky scissors to grab prey, such as moths or caterpillars.

◀ The mantis stays perfectly still, camouflaged by its body coloring, which blends in with the leaf or flower where it waits. When a victim comes near—SNAP!

QUIZ

1. What does a wasp use its jaws for?

2. Finish the name of this insect: praying...?

3. Which insect's larva digs small pits in sand?

Answers:
1. Digging and cutting up food
2. Mantis 3. Antlion

Veggie bugs

◀ Mealybugs, scale insects, and aphids can be serious pests in vegetable fields, orchards, and greenhouses.

41 About nine out of ten kinds of insects eat some kind of plant food. Many feed on soft, rich, nutritious substances. These include the sap in stems and leaves, the mineral-rich liquid in roots, the nectar in flowers, and the soft flesh of squashy fruits and berries.

▲ Most shield bugs feed on plant sap using their sucking mouthparts.

42 Solid wood may not seem very tasty, but many kinds of insects eat it. They usually consume the wood when they are larvae or grubs, making tunnels as they eat their way through trees, logs, and timber structures, such as bridges, fences, houses, and furniture.

► Woodworms are various kinds of wood-eating beetle larvae. Some stay in the wood for three years or more.

43 Animal droppings are delicious to many kinds of insects. Various types of beetles lay their eggs in warm, steamy piles of droppings. When the larvae hatch out, they eat the dung.

▲ Dung beetles mold soft dung into a ball shape. They roll the ball into a hole, which they have dug to lay their eggs in. The ball then covers their eggs.

◀ A lacebug jabs its sharp mouthparts into a plant to suck up the rich, syrupy sap inside.

44 Insects are not fussy eaters! They feed on old bits of damp and crumbling wood, dying trees, brown and decaying leaves, and smelly, rotting fruit. This is nature's way of recycling goodness and nutrients in old plant parts, and returning them to the soil so new trees and other plants can grow.

▲ Fruitworms are insect larvae that may be moth caterpillars or beetle grubs, as shown here.

Stings and things

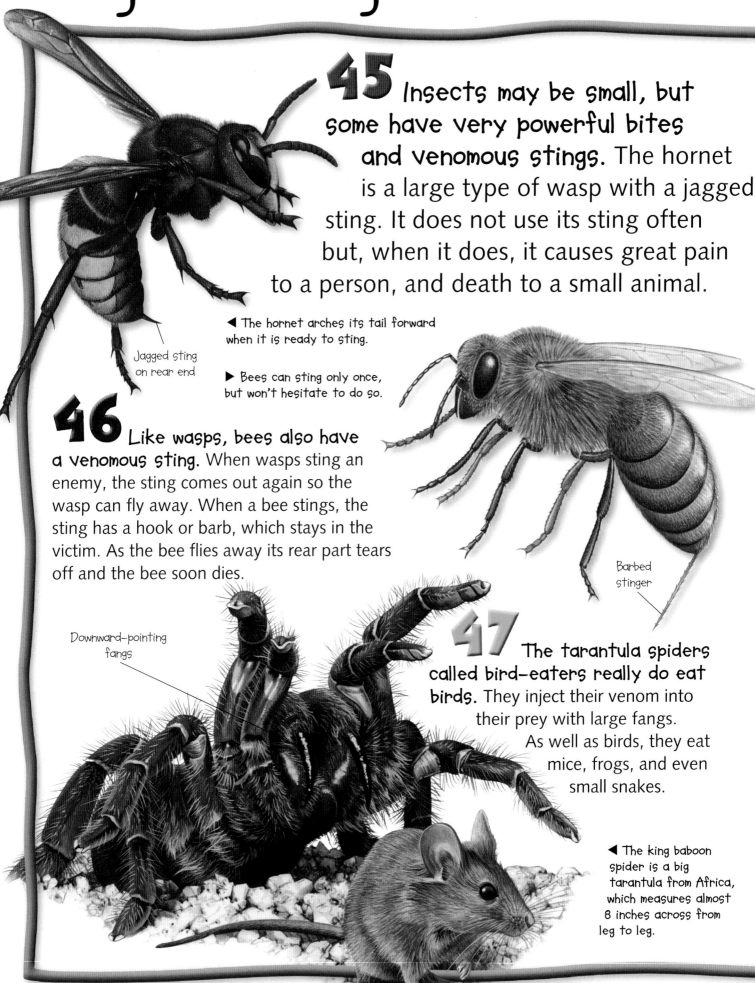

45 Insects may be small, but some have very powerful bites and venomous stings. The hornet is a large type of wasp with a jagged sting. It does not use its sting often but, when it does, it causes great pain to a person, and death to a small animal.

◀ The hornet arches its tail forward when it is ready to sting.

▶ Bees can sting only once, but won't hesitate to do so.

Jagged sting on rear end

46 Like wasps, bees also have a venomous sting. When wasps sting an enemy, the sting comes out again so the wasp can fly away. When a bee stings, the sting has a hook or barb, which stays in the victim. As the bee flies away its rear part tears off and the bee soon dies.

Barbed stinger

Downward-pointing fangs

47 The tarantula spiders called bird-eaters really do eat birds. They inject their venom into their prey with large fangs. As well as birds, they eat mice, frogs, and even small snakes.

◀ The king baboon spider is a big tarantula from Africa, which measures almost 8 inches across from leg to leg.

48 To startle and sting an attacker, the bombardier beetle squirts out a spray of hot liquid. It comes out of its rear end like a spray gun and gives the beetle time to escape.

QUIZ

1. What happens to a bee when it uses its sting?
2. Do bird-eating spiders really eat birds?
3. What does the bombardier beetle do to avoid attacks?

Answers:
1. It dies 2. Yes 3. It sprays hot liquid at its attacker

▼ Army ants march and feed by day, then gather in a clumplike "living nest" or bivouac to rest at night.

49 One army ant can give a small bite, but 10,000 ants are much more dangerous. Army ants are mainly from South America and do not stay in a nest like other ants. They march in long lines through the forest, eating whatever they can bite, sting, and overpower, from large spiders to lizards and birds.

Clever colonies

50 Some insects live together in huge groups called colonies, which are like insect cities. There are four main types of insects that form colonies. One is the termites. The other three are all in the same insect subgroup and are bees, wasps, and ants.

▶ An ants' nest is packed with tunnels and chambers.

51 Different kinds of ants make nests from whatever material is available. Ants might use mud, small sticks, and twigs, tiny bits of stone and gravel, or chewed-up pieces of leaves and flowers.

Winged males and females leave to start their own nests

52 Leafcutter ants grow their own food. They harvest leaves to use in the nest to grow fungi, which they eat.

53 In most insect colonies, only one or two members lay eggs. These are the queens and they are usually much bigger than the other ants. A queen can lay over 100 eggs each day.

Nursery chamber with ant larvae

The queen lays eggs in a separate chamber

▼ This wasp is making new cells for larvae.

54 A wasps' nest will have about 5,000 wasps in it, but these are small builders in the insect world! A termite colony may have more than 5,000,000 inhabitants! Wood ants form nests of up to 300,000. Honeybees number around 50,000, while bumblebees live in colonies of only 10 or 20.

I DON'T BELIEVE IT!

Ants look after aphids and milk them like cows! They stroke the aphids to obtain a sugary liquid called honeydew, which the ants sip to get energy.

Worker ants care for the eggs and larvae

55 Inside an ants' nest are many kinds of workers, each with different jobs to do. Foragers tunnel into the soil and collect food, such as bits of plants and animals. Guards at the entrances to the nest bite any animals that try to come in. Nursery workers look after the eggs, larvae, and pupae, while courtiers feed and clean the queen.

Where am I?

56 Insects have some of the best types of camouflage in the world. Camouflage is when a living thing blends in with its surroundings, so it is difficult to notice. This makes it hard for predators to see it. Or, if the insect is a predator, camouflage helps it to stalk its prey unnoticed.

57 The thornbug has a hard, pointed body casing. It sits still on a twig pretending to be a real thorn. It moves about and feeds at night.

▲ Thornbugs stay completely still during the daytime.

The "thorn" is part of the thorax

58 Shieldbugs have broad, flat bodies that look like leaves. The body is shaped like a shield carried by a medieval knight-in-armor.

◀ Shieldbugs stay on leaves of their own color.

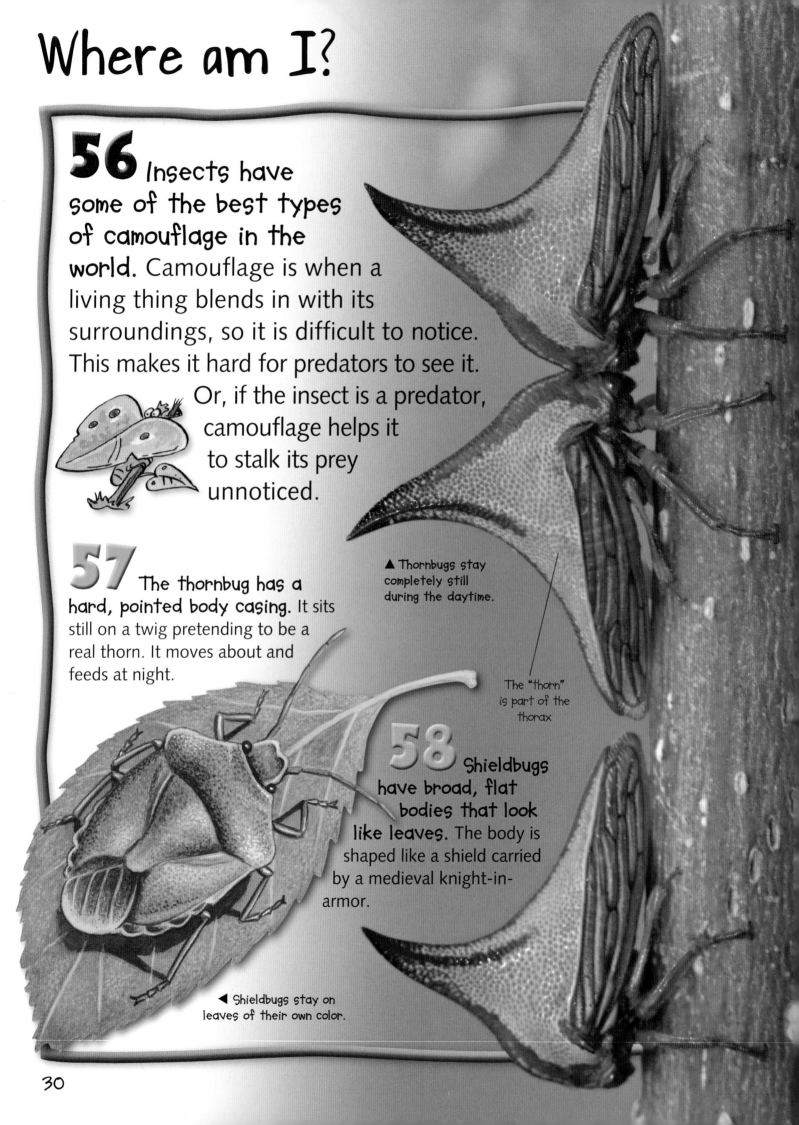

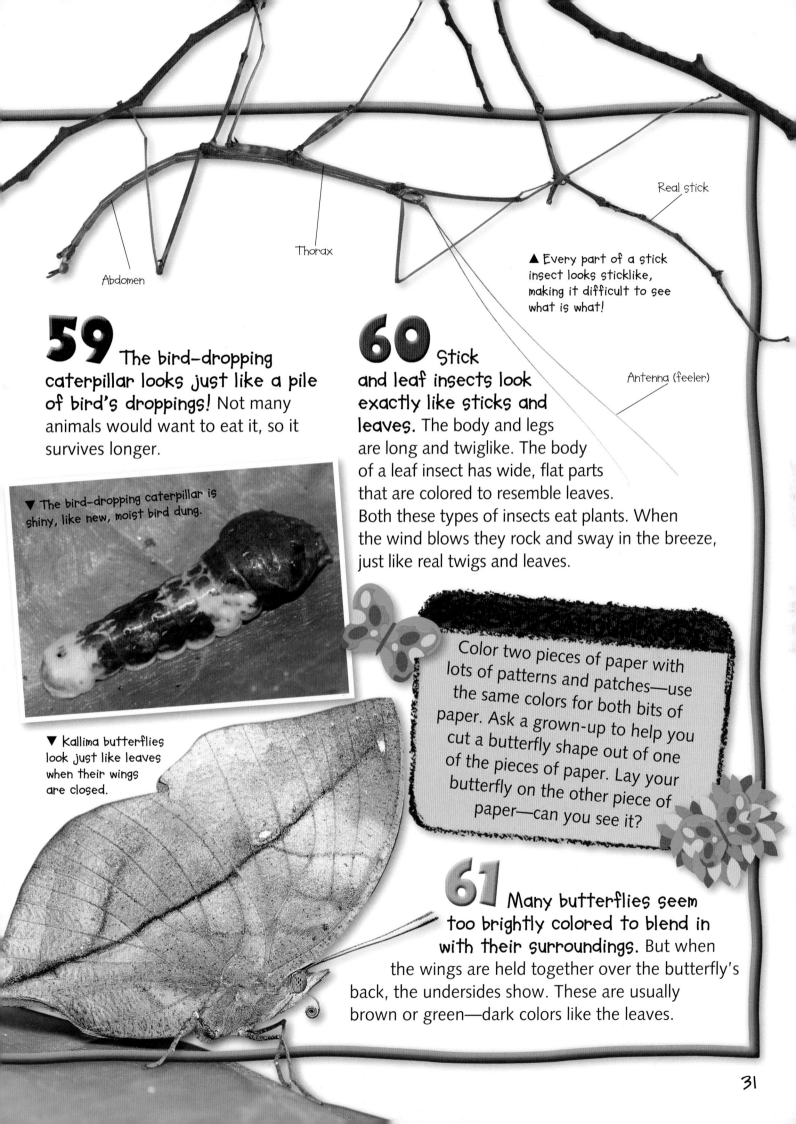

Real stick

Abdomen

Thorax

▲ Every part of a stick insect looks sticklike, making it difficult to see what is what!

Antenna (feeler)

59 The bird-dropping caterpillar looks just like a pile of bird's droppings! Not many animals would want to eat it, so it survives longer.

▼ The bird-dropping caterpillar is shiny, like new, moist bird dung.

60 Stick and leaf insects look exactly like sticks and leaves. The body and legs are long and twiglike. The body of a leaf insect has wide, flat parts that are colored to resemble leaves. Both these types of insects eat plants. When the wind blows they rock and sway in the breeze, just like real twigs and leaves.

Color two pieces of paper with lots of patterns and patches—use the same colors for both bits of paper. Ask a grown-up to help you cut a butterfly shape out of one of the pieces of paper. Lay your butterfly on the other piece of paper—can you see it?

▼ Kallima butterflies look just like leaves when their wings are closed.

61 Many butterflies seem too brightly colored to blend in with their surroundings. But when the wings are held together over the butterfly's back, the undersides show. These are usually brown or green—dark colors like the leaves.

Great pretenders

62 Some insects are shaped and colored to look like other animals. This can make them seem stronger or more dangerous, even when they are not. Pretending to be another animal is known as mimicry.

◀ The harmless hoverfly looks just like a wasp. Like other mimics, it fools other animals into thinking it is more dangerous than it is.

63 The animal pretending is called the mimic, the creature it looks like is called the model. Usually the model has a nasty sting, poisonous flesh, or some other feature that protects it from attack.

Antennae sense prey

Large eyes

◀ The ant beetle looks like the velvet ant, which has a painful sting.

Body pattern similar to velvet ant

64 The ant beetle resembles an ant. But it does not have a strong bite or sting like a real ant. The ant beetle enters the ants' nest and steals ant larvae to eat.

Monarch butterfly (model)

Viceroy butterfly (mimic)

65 The monarch butterfly has bright, bold colors on its wings. These warn other animals, such as birds and lizards, that its flesh tastes horrible and is poisonous. The viceroy butterfly looks very similar to the monarch, but its flesh is not distasteful.

▲ The viceroy butterfly is a mimic of the monarch butterfly.

▲ Hornet moths have colored wings, unlike real hornets.

66 The bee fly looks just like a bee. It has a hairy, striped body and can hover and hum like a bee, but it can't sting.

▶ The bee fly avoids predators by looking like a bee.

67 The hornet moth is a mimic of the large type of wasp known as the hornet. A hornet has a very painful sting and few other creatures dare to try and eat it. The hornet moth is harmless, but few other creatures dare to eat it either.

QUIZ

1. Can the bee fly sting?

2. Which butterfly looks similar to the monarch butterfly?

3. Which insect does a hoverfly look like?

Answers:
1. No
2. Viceroy butterfly 3. Wasp

33

Stay or go?

68 The cold of winter or the dryness of drought mean hard times for most animals, including insects. One way to survive is to hibernate. Many insects find a safe, sheltered place and go to sleep because they are too cold to move. Butterflies crawl behind creepers and vines. Ladybugs cluster in thick bushes. Beetles dig into the soil or among tree roots. As the weather becomes warmer, they become active again.

▼ Ladybugs gather in jumbled piles for winter.

69 In North America, monarch butterflies fly south during the fall. They migrate to warmer areas and millions of them gather in winter roosts. Next spring they all fly north again to feed and breed.

70 Some insects migrate the wrong way! In Australia, bogong moths sometimes fly off in search of better conditions. Some keep on flying over the sea, fall into the water and die.

71 Some insects migrate only when they become too numerous. After a few years of good conditions in Africa, locusts (a type of large grasshopper) increase in number so much they form vast swarms. With so many locusts together, they eat all the food in a whole area then fly off to look for more. They eat massive areas of farm crops and people are left to starve.

QUIZ

1. How do ladybugs keep warm in winter?
2. How many locusts can be in a swarm?
3. Why do some insects migrate long distances?

Answers:
1. Cluster in bushes
2. Billions 3. To find better conditions to help them survive

▲ Some locust swarms are so vast, with billions of insects, they take several days to fly past.

Noisy neighbors

72 The tropical forest is warm and still—but far from quiet. Many insects are making chirps, buzzes, clicks, screeches, hums, and other noises. Most are males, making their songs or calls to attract females at breeding time.

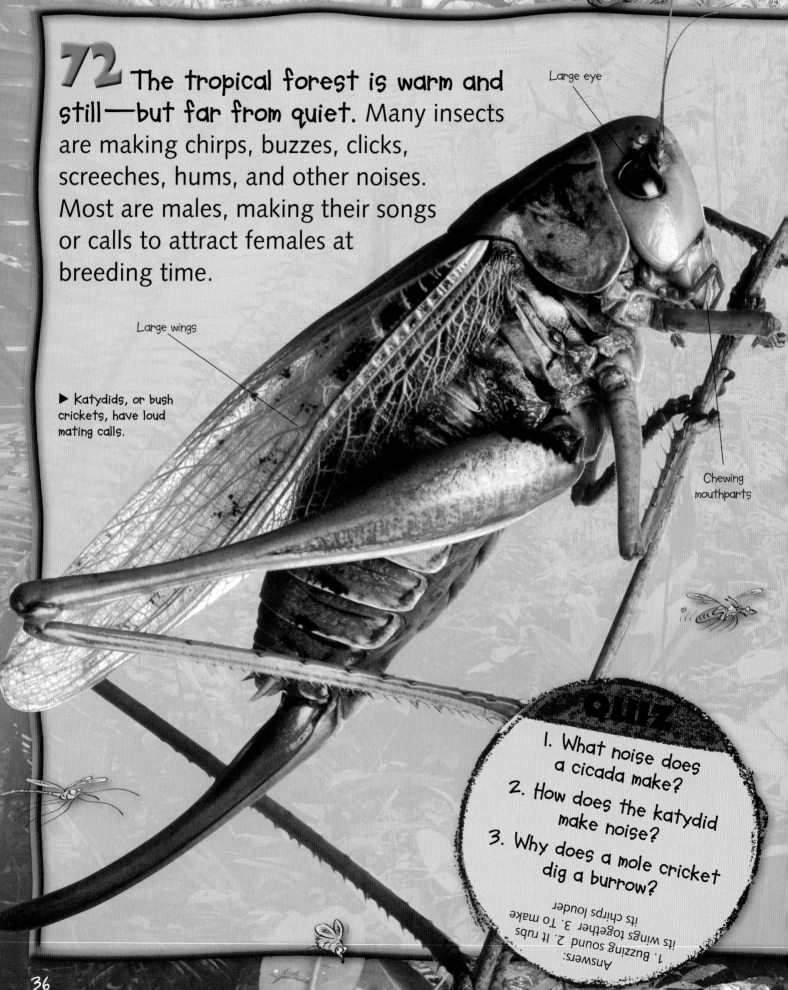

Large eye

Large wings

▶ Katydids, or bush crickets, have loud mating calls.

Chewing mouthparts

73 Some of the noisiest insects are cicadas, plant-eating bugs with large wings. The male cicada has two thin patches of body casing, called tymbals, one on either side of its abdomen (its rear body part). Tiny muscles pull in each patch, then let it go again, like clicking a tin lid in and out.

Air cavity (makes sounds louder)

Tymbal (sound-making patch)

Tymbal muscle

Compound eyes

Thorax

▶ A cicada's clicks are so fast, they merge into a buzzing sound, which can be heard more than half a mile away.

74 The male mole cricket chirps like a katydid. It sits at the entrance to its burrow in the soil. The entrance is shaped like a loudspeaker, so it makes the chirps sound louder and travel further.

▶ The mole cricket's song is heard 1.2 miles away.

75 Like most other crickets, the male katydid chirps by rubbing its wings together. The bases of the wings near the body have hard, ridged strips like rows of pegs. These click past each other to make the chirping sound.

Meet the family!

76 Are all minibeasts and bugs truly insects? One way to tell is to count the legs. If a creature has six legs, it's an insect. If it has more legs or fewer, it is some other kind of animal. Leg-counting works only with adult creatures.

QUIZ

1. How many legs does an insect have?

2. Is a woodlouse an insect or crustacean?

3. Which has more legs— a millipede or a centipede?

Answers:
1. Six 2. Crustacean 3. Millipede

Single left and right wings

Hard forewing cases called elytra

► Flies are insects with six legs and one set of wings.

Flying hindwings folded up under elytra

▲ The cardinal beetle is an insect with six legs and two sets of wings.

▼ The red spider mite has eight legs, like its cousins, the spiders.

Furry body

Feelers and mouthparts

77 Mites and ticks have eight legs, so they are not insects. Ticks, and some mites, cling onto larger animals and suck their blood. Some mites are so small that a handful of soil may contain half a million of them. Mites and ticks belong to the group of animals with eight legs, called arachnids. Other arachnids are spiders and scorpions.

78 A woodlouse has a hard body casing and feelers on its head. It has more than ten legs so it is certainly not an insect! It is a crustacean—a cousin of crabs and lobsters.

▲ Most woodlice have seven pairs of walking legs.

79 Millipedes have 50 or 100 legs, maybe even more. They are definitely not insects. Millipedes eat bits of plants, such as old leaves, bark, and wood.

Hard ringlike segment

Long front fangs

▲ A millipede has four legs on each body segment (section).

► A centipede has two legs on each body segment.

Extra long legs on last segment

80 A centipede has lots of legs, far more than six— usually over 30. It has two very long fangs, which gives it a venomous bite. It races across the ground hunting for insects to eat.

Silky spiders

81 A spider has eight legs, so it's not an insect—it is an arachnid. All spiders are deadly hunters. They have large fanglike jaws to grab and stab their prey. The fangs inject a venom to kill or quieten the victim. The spider then tears it apart and eats it, or sucks out its body juices. Scorpions, mites, and ticks have eight legs too, so they are also arachnids.

▶ This argiope spider has caught a grasshopper in its web. It wraps its prey in silk to stop it moving.

Several spinnerets produce silk

Spigots produce coarse silk for making webs

Spools produce fine silk for wrapping prey

Front legs wrap silk around prey

82 **All spiders can make thin, fine threads called silk.** These come out of spinnerets at the rear of the spider. About half of the 40,000 kinds of spiders make webs to catch prey. Some spiders make silk bags, called cocoons, to lay their eggs in or create protective "tents" for their young.

▶ The hardest part of building a web is getting the first thread in place. The spider needs a gust of wind to carry the thread across, so it sticks to a good spot.

① The first thread is horizontal

② The second thread makes a Y-shape

③ More strands, called radials, are added

④ A temporary spiral is put in place

⑤ The final spiral is built more carefully

83 **Some spiders use their silk threads in strange ways.** The spitting spider squirts sticky silk at its victim. The bolas spider creates a fishing line to catch insects flying past. The water spider makes a criss-cross sheet of silk to hold bubbles of air, which it needs in order to breathe underwater.

▼ The spitting spider spits a mixture of venom and "glue" at its prey.

Inventive arachnids

84 Not all spiders catch their prey using webs. Wolf spiders are strong and have long legs. They can run fast and chase tiny prey such as beetles, caterpillars, and slugs.

▶ The wolf spider stalks its prey, then makes a final rush at it.

The name "tarantula" was first given to a type of wolf spider from Europe. Its body is about 1.6 inches long and it lives in a burrow. Its bite can be very irritating and painful.

▼ The crab spider watches for prey with its eight small eyes.

85 The crab spider looks like a small crab, with a wide body and curved legs. It usually sits on a flower that is the same color as itself. It keeps very still so it is camouflaged. Small insects such as flies, beetles, and bees come to the flower to gather food and the crab spider pounces on them.

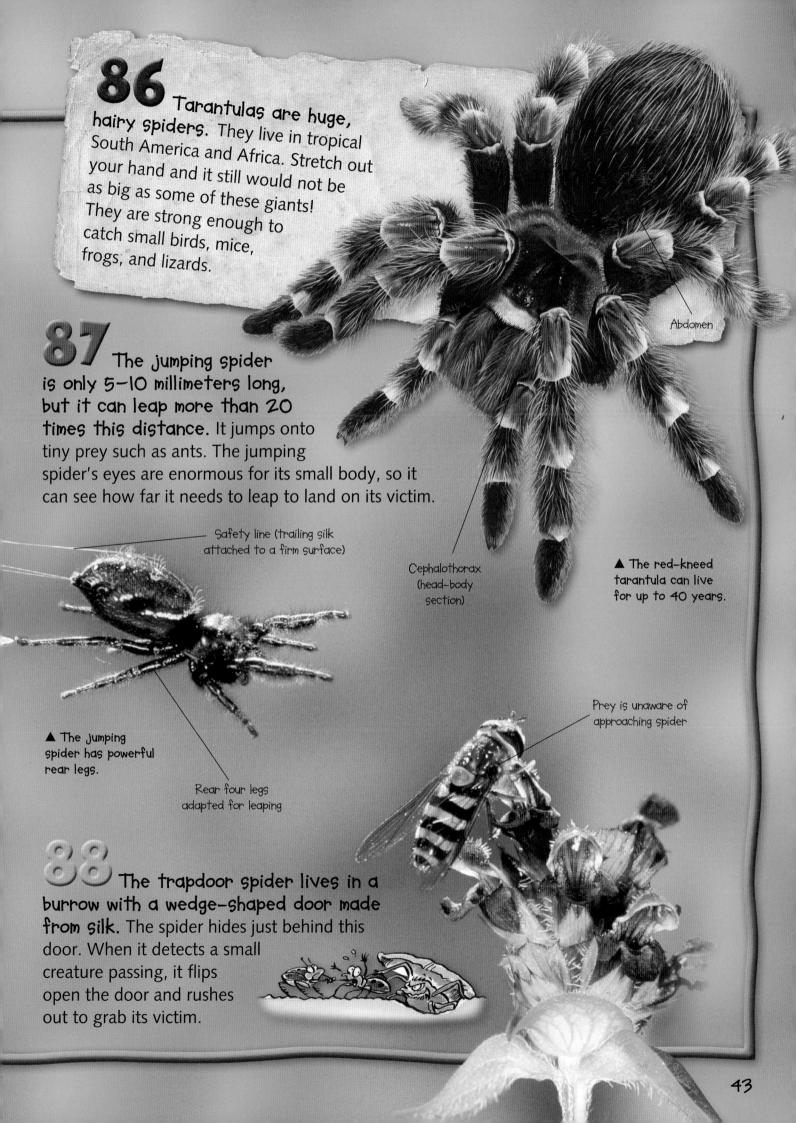

86 Tarantulas are huge, hairy spiders. They live in tropical South America and Africa. Stretch out your hand and it still would not be as big as some of these giants! They are strong enough to catch small birds, mice, frogs, and lizards.

87 The jumping spider is only 5–10 millimeters long, but it can leap more than 20 times this distance. It jumps onto tiny prey such as ants. The jumping spider's eyes are enormous for its small body, so it can see how far it needs to leap to land on its victim.

Abdomen

Cephalothorax (head-body section)

▲ The red-kneed tarantula can live for up to 40 years.

Safety line (trailing silk attached to a firm surface)

▲ The jumping spider has powerful rear legs.

Rear four legs adapted for leaping

Prey is unaware of approaching spider

88 The trapdoor spider lives in a burrow with a wedge-shaped door made from silk. The spider hides just behind this door. When it detects a small creature passing, it flips open the door and rushes out to grab its victim.

Deadly and dangerous

89 A scorpion has eight legs. Like a spider, it is an arachnid. Scorpions live in warm parts of the world. Some are at home in watery rain forests, others like hot deserts. The scorpion has large, crablike pincers called pedipalps to grab its prey, and powerful jaws like scissors to chop it up.

90 The scorpion has a dangerous venomous sting at the tip of its tail. It can use this to paralyze or kill a victim. The scorpion may also wave its tail at enemies to warn them that unless they go away, it will sting them.

Stinger on last tail part

▶ This scorpion is attacking a grasshopper.

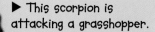

Pedipalp claws grab prey

91 The false scorpion looks like a scorpion with big pincers. It does not have a venomous sting in its tail—it does not even have a tail. It is tiny and could fit into this "O!" It lives in soil and hunts even smaller creatures.

▶ False scorpions hunt tiny bugs, as small as a full stop.

92 A crab may seem an odd cousin for a spider or scorpion. But the horseshoe or king crab is very unusual. It has eight legs—so it's an arachnid. It also has a large domed shell and strong spiky tail. There were horseshoe crabs in the seas well before dinosaurs roamed the land.

▶ Horseshoe crabs come onto the shore at breeding time.

93 The sun spider or solifuge is another very fierce, spiderlike hunter, although it has no venom. Most kinds live in deserts and are known as camel spiders.

94 Animals don't have to be big to be dangerous. These spiders are all very venomous and their bites can even kill people. This is why you should never mess about with spiders or poke your hands into holes or dark places!

The European black widow has up to 13 red patches on its abdomen

New Zealand's katipo is found along seashore dunes

The Australian redback has a body length of about 10 millimeters

QUIZ

1. Scorpions and spiders belong to which family group?
2. What does a scorpion use its tail for?
3. What is another name for a king crab?

Answers:
1. Arachnids 2. To paralyze the victim 3. Horseshoe crab

45

Friends and foes

95 Some insects are harmful —but others are very helpful. They are a vital part of the natural world. Flies, butterflies, beetles, and many other insects visit flowers to collect nectar and pollen to eat. In the process they carry pollen from flower to flower. This is called pollination and is needed so that the flower can form seeds or fruits.

Bee jaws chew and shape the wax cell walls

Bees communicate by antenna-stroking

96 Bees make honey from flower pollen and nectar. Honey is packed with energy, and bees use it to feed their larvae when conditions are bad. Their visits to flowers pollinate hundreds of kinds of our own food plants. People keep honeybees in hives so the honey is easier to collect.

◄ Honeybees store honey in six-sided compartments called cells, in layers known as honeycombs.

97 A few kinds of insects are among the most harmful creatures in the world. They do not attack and kill people directly, like tigers and crocodiles, but they do spread dangerous diseases, such as malaria.

I DON'T BELIEVE IT!
Most insects die from cold and lack of food in the winter. Before they die, they lay tiny eggs in sheltered places. Next year the eggs hatch and the yearly cycle of insect life begins again.

98 Mosquitoes spread diseases by blood-sucking. Their blood-filled bodies are also food for a huge range of animals, from dragonflies and centipedes to frogs, small birds, and shrews.

Abdomen held clear of skin

Antennae detect skin warmth

▶ A mosquito sucks blood from human skin.

Needlelike mouthparts in skin

▲ Spiders play a vital role in our ecosystem.

99 Spiders are very helpful to gardeners. They catch lots of insect pests, such as flies, in their webs.

100 Insects are so numerous and varied, they provide essential links to the food chains of almost every habitat. Countless small creatures eat insects who have eaten plants, then bigger animals eat the small creatures and so on. If insects disappeared, most other animal life would soon starve!

Index